Simply Inspirational

As we face the joys and challenges of life, we could all use a bit of inspiration from time to time. These words of wisdom bring a smile to our face, transform our thoughts, warm our hearts, and encourage our souls and spirits to soar. That's why we've assembled this heartwarming collection of ten cross stitch quotes. Chosen from among the best-loved designs published in the cherished magazine *For The Love Of Cross Stitch*, these needlework designs are suitable for a variety of occasions. So when the sluggishness of Monday morning comes a little too early or unexpected challenges make the day seem extra-long, let these inspiring quotations and lovely designs bring a smile to your face.

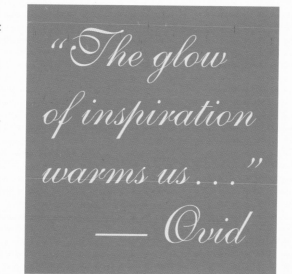

"The glow of inspiration warms us…"
— Ovid

LEISURE ARTS, INC
Little Rock, AR

Table of Contents

When Spring Comes 3

Garden Birdsong 6

Pure in Heart 8

"Believe on the Lord" 10

Pleasant Thoughts...11

God's Patchwork Angel 12

Give Thanks Sampler 14

"Jesus Loves Me!" 16

Marks of Praise...18

God's Almighty Hand 20

General Instructions...23

Framed by an engaging quote from Thomas Jones, this cozy, slice-of-life garden scene captures the essence of springtime hope and renewal. A puffed-up bird perched atop a shovel adds a touch of whimsy.

X	DMC	1/4X	B'ST	ANC.	COLOR
•	blanc	•		2	white
✖	319	◢	⁄	218	vy dk green
▦	320	◢		215	green
Π	341	◢		117	violet
✖	347	◢		1025	dk red
◔	367	◢		217	dk green
$	368	◢		214	lt green
•	369	•		1043	vy lt green
▦	420	◢		374	lt brown
◨	433			358	vy dk tan
2	434	2		310	dk tan
☐	435	◢		1046	tan
◇	436	◢		1045	lt tan
C	437	c		362	vy lt tan
■	502	◢		877	dk blue green
Π	503	◢		876	blue green
✧	504	◢		1042	lt blue green
■	519	◢		1038	turquoise
✖	552	◢		99	dk purple
▲	553	▲		98	purple
2	610	◢		889	vy dk khaki
☆	611	◢		898	dk khaki
✳	612	◢		832	khaki
♡	613	◢		831	lt khaki
☆	725	◢		305	dk yellow
$	726	◢		295	yellow
✔	813	✔		161	blue
★	825	◢		162	vy dk blue
H	826	H		161	dk blue
=	827			160	lt blue
■	924	◢		851	vy dk grey blue
P	926	P		850	grey blue
T	927	T		848	lt grey blue
✕	928	◢		274	vy lt grey blue
8	975	8		355	vy dk terra cotta
d	976	d		1001	terra cotta
✳	977	◢		1002	lt terra cotta
✧	3045	◇		888	dk beige
T	3046	T	⁄	887	beige
＼	3047	＼		852	lt beige
♥	3328	◢		1024	red
✦	3346	◢		267	dk yellow green
T	3347	◢		266	yellow green
＼	3348	◢		264	lt yellow green
◨	3371	◢	⁄	382	vy dk brown
◔	3687	◢		68	dk pink
✔	3688	✔		66	pink
△	3689	△		49	lt pink
■	3712	◢		1023	lt red
◎	3747			120	lt violet
▦	3761	◢		928	lt turquoise
5	3768	5		779	dk grey blue
■	3781	◢	⁄	1050	brown
✚	3826	◢		1049	dk terra cotta
%	3827	◢		311	vy lt terra cotta
◉	blanc				white French Knot
●	3371				vy dk brown French Knot
▨					Grey area indicates first row of right section of design.

147w x 120h

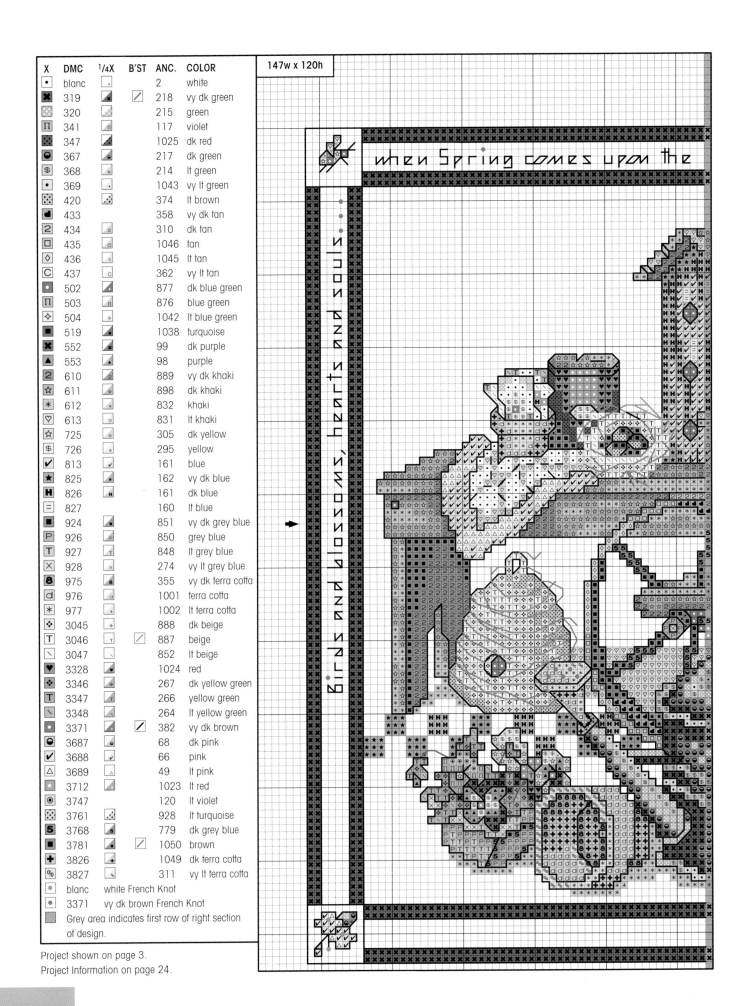

Project shown on page 3.
Project Information on page 24.

Design by Sandi Gore Evans.
Needlework adaptation by Lynn Busa.

world, all things are made new. ♡ Thomas

Jones

"SPRING"

The garden would
be very silent if
no birds sang there
except for those who
sang the best.
-Audubon

This charming little bird, paired with a delightful verse in Garden Birdsong, conveys Barbara Baatz' immense love of natural themes and gardening.

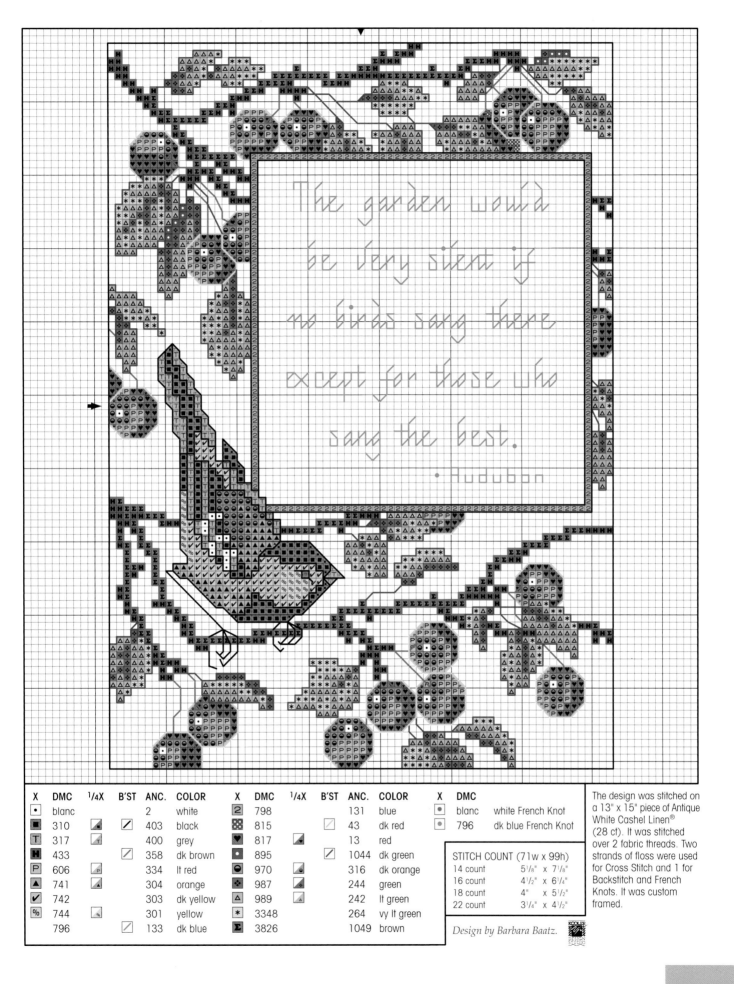

The garden would be very silent if no birds sang there except for those who sang the best.
• Audubon

Design by Barbara Baatz.

X	DMC	1/4X	B'ST	ANC.	COLOR	X	DMC	1/4X	B'ST	ANC.	COLOR	X	DMC		
•	blanc			2	white	2	798			131	blue	⊙	blanc		white French Knot
■	310	◢	✓	403	black	▦	815			43	dk red	⊙	796		dk blue French Knot
T	317	◪		400	grey	♥	817	◢		13	red				
H	433		✓	358	dk brown	●	895		✓	1044	dk green				
P	606	◿		334	lt red	◐	970	◢		316	dk orange				
▲	741	◢		304	orange	✤	987	◢		244	green				
✔	742			303	dk yellow	△	989			242	lt green				
%	744	◣		301	yellow	*	3348			264	vy lt green				
	796		✓	133	dk blue	Σ	3826			1049	brown				

STITCH COUNT (71w x 99h)

14 count	5 1/8"	x 7 1/8"
16 count	4 1/2"	x 6 1/4"
18 count	4"	x 5 1/2"
22 count	3 1/4"	x 4 1/2"

The design was stitched on a 13" x 15" piece of Antique White Cashel Linen® (28 ct). It was stitched over 2 fabric threads. Two strands of floss were used for Cross Stitch and 1 for Backstitch and French Knots. It was custom framed.

Delicate roses blooming beside a garden gate illustrate the lovely scripture from Matthew 5:8, "Blessed are the pure in heart; for they shall see God." The charming piece will make a special gift or an exquisite accent for your home.

STITCH COUNT (85w x 96h)

14 count	6⅛"	x	6⅞"
16 count	5⅜"	x	6"
18 count	4¾"	x	5⅜"
22 count	3⅞"	x	4⅜"

Blessed are, the pure in heart: for they shall see God. Mt. 5:8

X	DMC	¼X	½X	B'ST	ANC.	COLOR
⊡	blanc	⊡			2	white
▦	208	◪			110	purple
✱	210				108	lt purple
☆	301	◪			1049	rust
▲	319	◪		╱	218	dk green
▬	333	◪			119	violet
	356			╱	5975	dk peach
◆	367	◪	▨		217	green
○	368	◪			214	lt green
	420		✦		374	hazel brown
◕	433	◪			358	dk brown
★	434	◪			310	brown
▽	435	◪			1046	lt brown
✕	502	◪	▨		877	grey green
	550			╱	102	dk purple
■	561	◪			212	dk blue green
◈	562	◪			210	blue green
═	644	◪			830	lt grey
✕	758	◪			882	peach
−	776	◪			24	pink
△	822	◪			390	beige
✳	869	◪			944	dk hazel brown
⊡	899	⊡			52	dk pink
	3011			╱ *	846	olive
◉	3023	◪				grey
	3371					black brown
	3787			╱	382	dk grey
⦿	3371					black brown French Knot
●	3787					dk grey French Knot
				*		Use 2 strands of floss.

The design was stitched on a 13" x 14" piece of Cream Belfast Linen (32 ct). It was stitched over 2 fabric threads. Two strands of floss were used for Cross Stitch and 1 for Half Cross Stitch, Backstitch, and French Knots unless otherwise noted in the color key. It was custom framed.

Design by Paula Vaughan.
Needlework adaptation by Jane Chandler.

"Believe on The *Lord"*

Remind a friend of where to anchor her faith with this insightful little memento. The ark design and verse, accented by a sprinkling of bead "raindrops," makes a wonderful present to give hope to the heart of one you love.

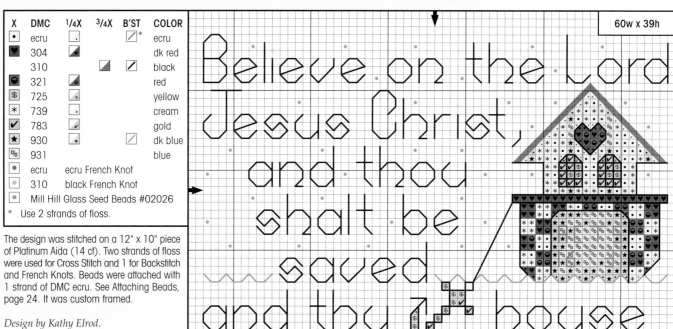

X	DMC	¹/4X	³/4X	B'ST	COLOR
•	ecru	.		✓*	ecru
♥	304	✓			dk red
	310		◣	✓	black
◒	321	◓			red
$	725	⑨			yellow
*	739	⁎			cream
✓	783	✓			gold
★	930	★		✓	dk blue
%	931				blue
•	ecru	ecru French Knot			
•	310	black French Knot			
•	Mill Hill Glass Seed Beads #02026				
*	Use 2 strands of floss.				

60w x 39h

The design was stitched on a 12" x 10" piece of Platinum Aida (14 ct). Two strands of floss were used for Cross Stitch and 1 for Backstitch and French Knots. Beads were attached with 1 strand of DMC ecru. See Attaching Beads, page 24. It was custom framed.

Design by Kathy Elrod.

Send a little birdie to remind a special family of the importance of keeping a positive attitude. Prettily framed, the uplifting design will add Nature's charm to any home.

X	DMC	1/4X	B'ST	ANC.
•	blanc			2
★	310		/	403
▲	400	◢	/	351
✖	415			398
◣	433			358
❖	435			1046
R	437			362
✚	502		/	877
H	504			1042
◔	725			305
⊠	775			128
◖	898			360
4	921			1003
%	3345		/	268
8	3347			266
◆	3348			264
Ø	3755		/	140
P	3773			1008
♥	3827	◞		311
•	310	black French Knot		

STITCH COUNT	(77w x 48h)
14 count	5½" x 3½"
16 count	4⅞" x 3"
18 count	4⅜" x 2¾"
22 count	3½" x 2¼"

The design was stitched on a 13" x 11" piece of Zweigart® Ivory Aida (16 ct). Two strands of floss were used for Cross Stitch and 1 for Backstitch and French Knot. It was inserted in a frame courtesy of East Side Mouldings (4½ x 6½ – 2300PM).

Design by Jorja Hernandez.

Beaming with a rosy countenance, our homespun guardian displays a divinely pieced friendship quilt. The collage of patchwork hearts is also the inspiration for this grandmotherly angel's benevolent counsel.

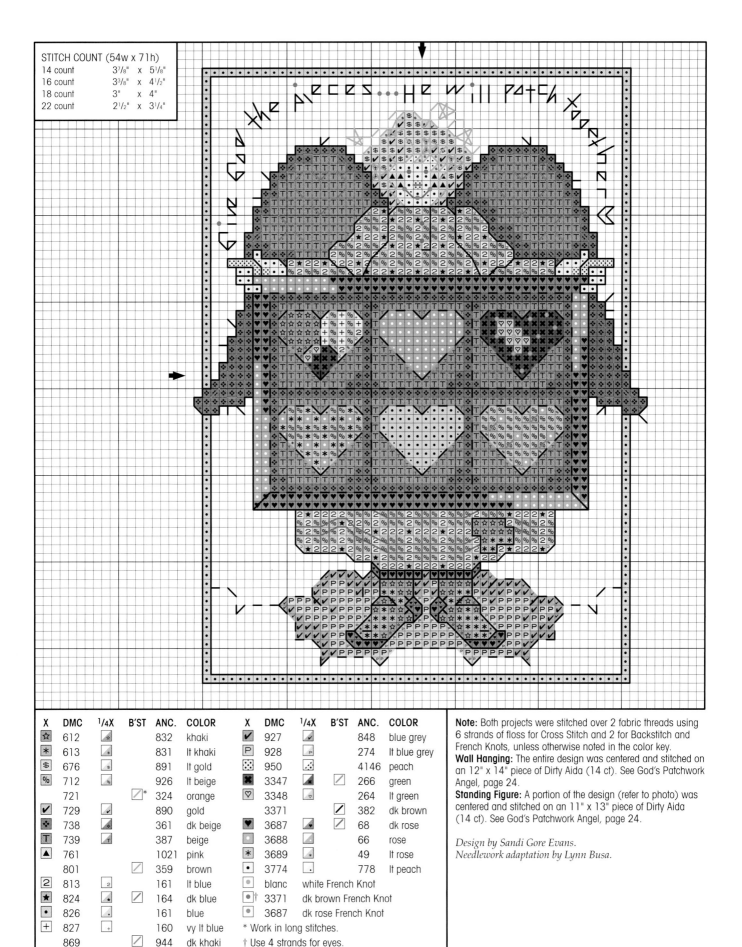

STITCH COUNT (54w x 71h)

14 count	3⅞"	x	5⅛"
16 count	3⅜"	x	4½"
18 count	3"	x	4"
22 count	2½"	x	3¼"

X	DMC	¼X	B'ST	ANC.	COLOR
☆	612			832	khaki
*	613			831	lt khaki
$	676			891	lt gold
%	712			926	lt beige
	721		⁄*	324	orange
✔	729			890	gold
✿	738			361	dk beige
T	739			387	beige
▲	761			1021	pink
	801		⁄	359	brown
2	813			161	lt blue
★	824		⁄	164	dk blue
•	826			161	blue
+	827			160	vy lt blue
	869		⁄	944	dk khaki

X	DMC	¼X	B'ST	ANC.	COLOR
✔	927			848	blue grey
P	928			274	lt blue grey
⠿	950			4146	peach
✖	3347		⁄	266	green
♡	3348			264	lt green
	3371		⁄	382	dk brown
♥	3687		⁄	68	dk rose
▫	3688			66	rose
*	3689			49	lt rose
•	3774			778	lt peach
▫	blanc				white French Knot
•†	3371				dk brown French Knot
•	3687				dk rose French Knot

* Work in long stitches.
† Use 4 strands for eyes.

Note: Both projects were stitched over 2 fabric threads using 6 strands of floss for Cross Stitch and 2 for Backstitch and French Knots, unless otherwise noted in the color key.

Wall Hanging: The entire design was centered and stitched on an 12" x 14" piece of Dirty Aida (14 ct). See God's Patchwork Angel, page 24.

Standing Figure: A portion of the design (refer to photo) was centered and stitched on an 11" x 13" piece of Dirty Aida (14 ct). See God's Patchwork Angel, page 24.

Design by Sandi Gore Evans.
Needlework adaptation by Lynn Busa.

13

Give your favorite hostess something special to be thankful for this Thanksgiving! She'll love the appearance of her holiday table when it's dressed up with these seasonal place mats and napkin rings. They're stitched with portions of the sampler, which makes a thoughtful year-round reminder that the time is always right for counting blessings.

X	DMC	ANC.	COLOR
#	309	42	red
★	472	253	lt green
◄	722	323	orange
■	743	302	yellow
▨	840	379	lt brown

X	DMC	ANC.	COLOR
▨	913	204	green
◥	938	381	dk brown
C			

Grey area indicates last row of top section of design.

Design by Deborah Lambein.

STITCH COUNT (51w x 156h)

14 count	3³/₄" x 11¹/₄"
16 count	3¹/₄" x 9³/₄"
18 count	2⁷/₈" x 8³/₄"
22 count	2³/₈" x 7¹/₈"

Note: All projects were stitched using 2 strands of floss for Cross Stitch.

Framed Piece: The entire design was stitched on a 12" x 19" piece of Zweigart® Antique White Cashel Linen® (28 ct). It was stitched over 2 fabric threads. It was custom framed.

Placemat: A portion of the design (refer to photo) was stitched in one corner of a Charles Craft, Inc.® White Royal Classic (14 ct) Placemat, 4 squares from the beginning of fringe.

Napkin Ring: A portion of the design (refer to photo) was stitched on a 10" x 6" piece of Charles Craft, Inc.® White Aida (14 ct). Repeat design as desired. It was made into a napkin ring.

For napkin ring, center design and trim stitched piece to measure 8" x 4".

Matching right sides and long edges, fold stitched piece in half. Use ¹/₄" seam allowance to sew long edges together. Trim seam allowance to ¹/₈" and turn stitched piece right side out. With seam centered in back, press stitched piece flat. Press short edges ¹/₂" to wrong side. Blind stitch short edges together.

Like children singing the familiar Sunday-school tune, these innocent lambs delight in exploring God's wondrous creation. The custom-framed design offers a gentle reminder of Jesus' love, and the top portion makes a sweet accent.

STITCH COUNT (77w x 100h)			
14 count	5½"	x	7¼"
16 count	4⅞"	x	6¼"
18 count	4⅜"	x	5⅝"
22 count	3½"	x	4⅝"

Jesus loves me! This I know, For the Bible tells me so.

X	DMC	¼X	B'ST	ANC.	COLOR	X	DMC	¼X	B'ST	ANC.	COLOR
•	blanc	.		2	white		801		⟋	359	brown
◼	326		⟋	59	dk pink		936		⟋	269	dk olive
⊕	451 &	⬟		233	grey &	H	956			40	pink
	452			232	lt grey	◼	957			50	lt pink
⊙	453	⊙		231	vy lt grey	⊕	963	⊕		73	vy lt pink
✤	504	⬟		1042	vy lt green	✳	977	✳		1002	lt golden brown
✖	700	◩		228	dk yellow green	⊞	3012			844	olive
⊠	702	⬕		226	yellow green	(	3013			842	lt olive
∷	704	∴		256	lt yellow green	★	3799		⟋	236	dk grey
○	772	○		259	vy lt yellow green	Ⅱ	3813	◢		875	lt green
	797		⟋	132	dk blue	✺	3816			876	green
◲	799	◩		136	blue	◼	3818	◢	⟋	923	dk green
#	800	#		144	lt blue		3826		⟋	1049	golden brown

Note: Both projects were stitched using 2 strands of floss for Cross Stitch and 1 for Backstitch.
Framed Piece: The entire design was stitched on a 14" x 15" piece of Zweigart® White Cashel Linen (28 ct). It was stitched over 2 fabric threads. It was custom framed.
Standing Figure: A portion of the design (refer to photo) was stitched on a 9" x 7" piece of Zweigart® White Aida (14 ct). It was made into a standing figure. To complete figure, see Standing Figure Finishing, page 24.

Design by Barbara Baatz.

KOOLER
DESIGN
STUDIO

17

To mark your daily prayers in reading The Good Book, turn to these oversized page keepers. Rich linen sets the tone for their inspiring words and traditional designs.

Each design was stitched on a 6" x 11" piece of Zweigart® Summer Khaki Belfast Linen (32 ct). They were stitched over 2 fabric threads. Two strands of floss were used for Cross Stitch and 1 for Backstitch and French Knots. They were made into bookmarks.

For each bookmark, trim stitched piece ³/₄" larger than design on all sides. Cut a piece of Summer Khaki Belfast Linen the same size as stitched piece for backing. Matching right sides and leaving an opening for turning, use a ¹/₂" seam allowance to sew fabric pieces together. Trim seam allowances diagonally at corners. Turn bookmark right side out, carefully pushing corners outward. Blind stitch opening closed; press bookmark flat.

Designs by Diane Williams.

X	DMC	B'ST	ANC.	COLOR	X	DMC	ANC.	COLOR
•	ecru	╱	387	ecru	★	3023	1040	grey
◎	355		1014	terra cotta	■	3051	681	dk olive green
◆	420		374	brown	T	3052	262	olive green
□	729		890	gold	▬	3345	268	green
%	758		882	peach	2	3346	267	lt green
8	869	╱	944	dk brown	♥	3787	273	dk grey
▣	895		1044	dk green	Ⅱ	3828	373	lt brown
◣	918		341	dk copper	•	3371	382	brown black
Σ	930		1035	dk blue				French Knot
Π	931		1034	blue				

Nostaglic silhouettes in a variety of rustic colors highlight the work ethic, perseverance, and faith of the old-time pioneers and settlers. Frame and display this inviting piece in its entirety or stitch block designs on frayed coasters to create a collection that will complement any country décor.